Sheepdog Max

words by Nigel Croser
illustrated by Neil Curtis

"Uh, oh," said Min and Mop.

"Here comes the sheepdog.

We'll have to run."

"I like to run," said Max.

The sheepdog chased the sheep.

So Max chased the sheepdog.

"This is fun," said Max.

The sheepdog ran around the sheep.

So Max ran between the sheep.

The sheep ran everywhere.

"This is fun," said Max.

The sheepdog ran behind the sheep.
So Max ran behind the sheepdog.
The sheep ran into the yard, and the
farmer shut the gate.

The sheepdog ran across the sheep.

He ran over their backs.

So Max ran over their backs, too.

"This is fun," said Max.

11

The sheepdog jumped onto the gate. So Max jumped onto the gate. Then the gate swung open and bumped the fence.

The sheepdog fell off and bumped the farmer.

The sheep ran out of the yard.

Max ran around the sheep.

Then he chased them back to the grass.

"It's fun being a sheepdog,"
said Max.

"You're not a sheepdog," said Min.

"You're a sheep sheep," said Mop.